(un)wrinkled

Gabriella DeBono

BookLeaf
Publishing

India | USA | UK

Presentation by *BookLeaf Publishing*

Web: www.bookleafpub.com

E-mail: info@bookleafpub.com

ISBN : 9789357447560

First edition 2021

DEDICATION

Thank you to my family, friends, and boyfriend for always supporting my writing. This book exists because you never stopped believing in me.

ACKNOWLEDGEMENT

All events described by the author are fictitious.

you

you
you are here
you are where you need to be
safe
from the race
there is no pace you need to keep

you
are
here.

(un)tangled

take a walk inside your tangles
eat your morning cereal across from them at the
breakfast table
let them sip on your extra sweet coffee and
butter your toast
let them pull your knit sweater over your collar
bones and apply your scarlet lipstick
tell them your favourite words and what tickles
your intestines
but don't let them in your room at night
they'll curl around your pillow and rock you to
sleep.

take a walk inside your tangles that are
winding yesterday into tomorrow.
they'll drown you if you can't swallow that
last time, that
last knot
you still can't
untangle.

take your tangles for a walk
run your fingers through them
watch the sun weave through the leaves of that
maple tree

lean your back into the trunk
let it support you
fall asleep with yourself

fall asleep with yourself.

everything

the sun is always there
even on the worst of days and
rain can bring you butterflies because
grey skies are all that really exist
when everything
is everything.

cannon ball

her freckles shimmer in the sun like a
swimming pool on a summer day.

she splashes the hot cement with a cannon ball,
I stall walking down the stairs,
wincing when the water reaches my belly
button.

her head reaches above the surface with
strawberry brown hair in her eyes.

water ends up in mine.

her laugh sounds like her crooked front tooth.
mine sounds like forgetting the water is cold.

~

her laugh changed when she got braces.
her hair isn't strawberry brown anymore

and yet,

I started doing cannon balls
hoping to hear my

favourite summer song
again.

in theory

we are loose notes
in a song we don't know how to
sing.

check your vitals

cotton candy skies and
most things sensationalized
we exist in nostalgic hyperbole
deaf to the piano that plays the
taste of home.

waiting for the bus

(you're) not less
just condensed (in me)
the wind feels like you today and I
forgot to take pictures of the flowers

(again).

honey

life showed me that it's capable of
drowning me in honey so I thought I could
breathe
but really, I was drowning in the worst parts of
me
it felt like a drug to be happy and
sad and mad and lost and leaving but never
coming home

you were merely a stop on the road

a romanticized bed to lay my head
when I couldn't face my life
or find peace at night
we became each other's reason to sleep
to sink
into honey and comfort and
a world where we didn't have to think

we could be
exactly what the other didn't need
it was magic and grief
never trust, but lust
we were sinking

in a pool of honey and magic and
never thinking.

one day I tried tell you I was gasping for air
and it didn't cross my mind
you didn't know how to save me
because if you did
you would've saved yourself.

it was fate
or a plan
that I let you be the ground where I used to stand
and
yell and fight and love and fall.

it was more than just scraped knees this time.

it was a hole that I didn't know how to find
how to fill

I left thinking someone new never will
make me feel like drowning in honey again

I was right.

I found someone who I can't always sleep beside
but in the afternoon
they're still holding my hand

and when it's hard they try to understand
and so do I.

we never did that
and I'll never know why.

I know we did the best that we could
and maybe that wasn't even close to good but,

it was fine for two kids who were drowning.
It was fine for two kids who were drowning.

it's not supposed to
make sense

yet for never maybe
we are never a now

Begin again

6 am saw me.

she offered her glowing grey

and morning dew.

anxiety

15

my third coffee feels like an unmade bed and my bleeding lips taste like I will never believe in myself in time.

tomorrow shows up

the clouds still cradle the
sky at the end of each day

it is just today
it is just today.

i'll fly on my own

there is endless latitude
that will never know I chased the
breeze for its secrets even when it was
holding nothing against its chest.

maybe that can be
my nuance.

say this on a sunday morning

I dare you to purposefully forget
forget the shape of your stomach and your
silhouette
feel yourself where you are instead
I promise you'll be okay if you forget.

(meaning)

it was someone's birthday
I watched their balloon
60th
disappear into the
fading blue sky painted with
summer whimsy

the espresso swallowed my hangover and
lust to create meaning

it was easy to float through the
small above-ground pool
it was easy to watch the balloon
shrink away

this isn't a poem about letting go.

it was just a balloon. I was just floating.

it was just summer and the blue sky.

a poem is not a butterfly

I'm sorry I'm not your butterfly
I just write things down.

but if I was,

I would tickle your cheek and
remind you to care about where you are
at this moment because

you'll never be here again.

budding

budding budding budding to be
everything plumpish and dainty and
delightfully no one's
the wrinkle between elegance and defeat
is where I exist

you wont go under

slow mud-pit sinking
I strain my chin up so I can still breathe
the sun burns my eyes
the dirt depths tug at my ankle bones.

I want to kick
struggle through the viscous gravity
I don't want to find the bottom
that only pulls me deeper

I surrender to the sludge

let it caress my neck like a feather-filled pillow
my toes peek through the surface
my body parallel with the horizon line

moving one finger at a time
I gently wade to shore
a sort of beached mud-cake
I crust over.

whimsy vs. defeat

I strung myself along
with imaginary synapses
running out of air like
flat tires
drifting into fantasy
and stars
dead since I learned
my name.

here

I think the thing I expected the least was
how much I would ache for the safety of
eighteen
the ecstasy of feeling everything
crumble like a block tower made by a toddler
I'd get up and do it all over again
high on coming-of-age movies, wavering faith
and the option of nothing being
off the table.

now, there's a clunky absence of
sadness and vastness

I stumble over my happiness.

magic doesn't taste like melancholy
life is more than my collapse.

just call the stars
freckled lights

we are always existing
there's no rush to find now
the sky is always leaving us
we are always walking home.